I HAVE A FRIEND
WITH LEARNING DISABILITIES

HANNAH CARLSON, M.ED., C.R.C.
DALE CARLSON

illustrated by
Richard Ambrose Kinrade

CHANEY SHANNON PRESS
BICK PUBLISHING HOUSE
MADISON, CT

Edited by Ann Maurer

With thanks to Kathleen C. Laundy, Psy.D., M.S.W.,
Clinical Instructor, Yale School of Medicine

CHANEY SHANNON PRESS is a trademark of
BICK PUBLISHING HOUSE

Library of Congress Catalog Card Number: 96-084059
ISBN: 1-884158-12-9 — Volume 5
ISBN: 1-884158-11-0 — 6 Volume Set

Printed by Royal Printing Service, USA

SPECIAL NEEDS/DISABILITIES

"A practical guide for general audiences who want to learn about disabilities in terms we can all understand."
— Kathleen C. Laundy, Psy.D., M.S.W.,
Yale School of Medicine

"Excellent introductory handbooks about disabilities and special needs. They discuss medical conditions and rehabilitation, feelings and adaptive technology, and responsible attitudes both on the part of people with disabilities and people temporarily without them. The emphasis is on our common humanity, not our differences."
— Lynn McCrystal, M.ED., vice-president,
The Kennedy Center

"The books offer professional information in an easy-to-use, uncomplicated style."
— Renee Abbott, Group Home Director,
S.A.R.A.H., Shoreline Association for
the Retarded and Handicapped

"Excellent, very informative."
— Alan R. Ecker, M.D., Assistant Clinical
Professor of Ophthalmology, Yale University

"These books are an important service. They are informed, practical guides to feelings, behavior patterns, medical facts, technology, and resources for people who care about people with disabilities."
— Richard Fucci, former president of the
National Spinal Cord Injury Association

ACKNOWLEDGMENTS

Our gratitude to Kathleen C. Laundy, Psy.D., M.S.W., Yale Child Study Center, Yale School of Medicine; to Renee Abbott, Group Home Director, S.A.R.A.H., the Shoreline Association of the Retarded and Handicapped; to Richard Fucci, former president of the National Spinal Cord Injury Association; to Alan Ecker, M.D., Assistant Clinical Professor of Ophthalmology of Yale University; to Jane Chamberlin, parent and employment supervisor, West Haven Community House; and to Lynn McCrystal, M.Ed., vice-president, The Kennedy Center, for their counsel and editorial advice.

Our gratitude to Louis and Susan Weady, not only for Royal Printing, but for their guidance and patience with new editions, purchase orders, and shipping.

Our gratitude to Bonnie Burke, for tender care of our accounts.

Our special thanks to Danny Carlson for teaching us how to use computer capabilities for publishing.

And our thanks to Terrence Finnegan for providing Bick Publishing House with its own computer system.

CONTENTS

1.   Conditions and Causes

2.   Their Feelings and Reactions,
      Your Feelings and Reactions

3.   Manners and Coping Aids: Both Sides

4.   Seeking Diagnosis

5.   Living with Learning Disabilities: Life Stories

6.   Resources: Special Education; IDEA and ADA;
      Support Systems and Services

7.   Other Conditions: Sensory Disorders;
      Communication Disorders; Autism; Antisocial
      Personality Disorder; The Gifted Child

Appendix: Sources for Help
            References
            Recommended Reading

NOTE

This book is an introduction to the world of people with learning disabilities, both children and adults. You know who they are: they're the ones you think of as not living up to their potential; who bounce from one school or relationship, profession or job to another; people who may have made it, who are creative and talented, but who are still driven, disorganized, impulsive — who act odd.

If you are friend, family, or interested in possible symptoms of your own, here are some basic understandings:

- people with learning disabilities do not have mental retardation

- emotional disturbances are secondary, not the cause

- learning disabilities is a general term that refers to difficulties in processing information due to a neurological disorder; that is, a dysfunction of the central nervous system—it's a physical, not an environmental, cause; hardware, not software, that is the problem

- learning disabilities are life disabilities — many last a whole lifetime, and they may interfere with work, school, family and social relationships

- learning disabilities are not caused by emotional and psychological difficulties, but self-image difficulties, disorientation, and emotional distress often result

- learning disabilities are hidden disabilities — people tend to disbelieve what they cannot see

- **seek help: learning disabilities can be diagnosed and helped**

A lot of people had and have learning disabilities: Mozart, Hans Christian Anderson, Einstein, U. S. presidents among them. Learning disabilities haven't kept doctors, lawyers, athletes, business people, writers, scientists from great success. Learning disabilities have not kept one of the authors of this book from a lifetime of writing books.

What is essential is to identify the problem and get help so that the disability doesn't overcome the abilities and waste a life.

1

CONDITIONS AND CAUSES

There are people, adults and children, who have learned to live successfully and yet know there is something wrong with them. People with learning disabilities are conscious of a missing piece, a glitch in the way they function. They just don't know what it is that makes them so good at what they're good at, and a disaster at something else.

And until recently, there was no way to measure accurately their strengths and weaknesses.

In the past, when people had a learning disorder, they were often grouped together without distinguishing their problems, or were warehoused with people who were emotionally disturbed or who had mental retardation.

There is still confusion today between mental retardation (significantly subaverage general intellectual functioning), mental illness (psychological disorders not due to below average intellectual functioning), and learning disabilities (one or more physically impaired systems not linked to intellectual functioning).

The establishment of three learning disabilities research centers at Yale, Johns Hopkins University, and the University of Colorado has been crucial in aiding people with learning disabilities. As a result of their research, the learning disability category has become the fastest-growing category within special education — special education not only at the elementary level, but among adults who wish to begin or continue adult education. With the new diagnostic techniques, the new adaptive and organizational aids, new medications, new attitudes, come new beginnings for all who are affected with the various categories of learning disabilities.

Because abbreviations are so often used here and elsewhere, the following are brief definitions of the major categories.

LD: LEARNING DISABILITY, an impaired language-processing problem

NLD: NONVERBAL LEARNING DISABILITY, impaired visual/motor processing, may include impaired social skills

ADHD: ATTENTION-DEFICIT HYPERACTIVITY DISORDER, impaired ability to focus attention; distractibility, impulsivity, restlessness

ADD: ATTENTION-DEFICIT DISORDER, same as above without the hyperactive component

WHAT IS A LEARNING DISABILITY (LD)?

Learning Disability Defined

The term 'learning-disabled' refers to people, children and adults, who fail to learn despite a tested normal capacity for learning, who display a defined <u>discrepancy</u> between the capacity to learn and actually learning, between intelligence test scores and achievement test scores, between *potential* and *performance*. **It is this wide gap that indicates a learning disability.**

The Wide Gap

The term does not refer to people whose difficulties in learning are due to blindness, deafness, mental retardation (a low level of intelligence), or environmental deprivation, or even to people with other disorders such as mental illness.

Federal law, under the Education for All Handicapped Children Act, provides the following description of a learning disability: "Specific learning disability means a disorder in one or more of the basic...processes in understanding or using language, spoken or written....[an] imperfect ability to listen, think, speak, read, write, spell, or do mathematical calculations." Federal guidelines state that there must be a 20-point discrepancy between I.Q. test scores and achievement tests scores. Using this definition, it is estimated that learning disability affects at least 10% of the U.S. population.

In 1989, the National Joint Committee on Learning Disabilities offered a definition that included people of all ages and added a social component.

Learning Disabilities is a general term that refers to a heterogeneous group of disorders manifested by significant difficulties in the acquisition and use of listening, speaking, reading, writing, reasoning, or mathematical abilities. These disorders are intrinsic to the individual, presumed to be due to central nervous system dysfunction, and may occur across the life span. Problems in self-regulatory behaviors, social perception, and social interaction may exist with learning disabilities but do not by themselves constitute a learning disability. Although learning disabilities may occur concomitantly with other handicapping conditions (for example, sensory impairment, mental retardation, serious emotional disturbance) or with...influences (such as cultural differences, insufficient or inappropriate instruction), they are <u>not the result of those conditions or influences.</u>

The Diagnostic and Statistical Manual of Mental Disorders-IV (DSM-IV) says: Learning Disorders are diagnosed when the individual's achievement on individually administered, standardized tests in reading, mathematics, or written expression is substantially below that expected for age, schooling, and level of intelligence. Because learning disabilities are basically information processing problems (word-blindness or instruction-deafness is not due to literal blindness or deafness, but a probably inherited, biological, nervous system disorder), they can be classified into two general groups.

Two Groups of Learning Disabilities

1.   those which involve auditory-verbal processes, resulting in reading disorders and other language-based learning problems (sometimes called dyslexia) — these impaired language-processing skills create problems in understanding written material, memory of written material, often difficulty in understanding what is heard

2.   those which involve visual and motor (nonverbal) processes, resulting in poor handwriting, difficulties in math, and/or deficits in social skills, lack of social judgment

Dr. Larry Silver, clinical professor of psychiatry, describes what the brain must do in order for learning to take place. The first step, he says, is **input** — getting the information into the brain from the eyes and ears. Second is **integration** — the brain needs to organize and make sense out of the information. Third, the **memory process** — the brain needs to store and to be able to retrieve the information. Finally, fourth, the brain needs to send messages back to the nerves and muscles to **output** the information. Learning disabilities may occur in any or all of the steps, from perception to processing, from memory to reason, logic, performance. And these can occur in academic subjects, or daily living skills that include everything from reading a shopping list to balancing a checkbook; from exercising social insight and reasoning, to the perception and awareness of the environment. There can be a kind of visual and social dyslexia as well as verbal and hearing dyslexia. The variety of ways the brain can scramble information or simply be deaf/blind to it is extraordinary. Here are some examples.

- your loved one, child, or friend can read, but can't remember what has been read

- misses hearing half of the instructions, forgets the other half

- speaks brokenly, leaves sentences incomplete, writes some letters backwards, has trouble making sense out of written material

- can see precisely enough to be an accomplished artist, but can't remember what has been seen in a movie a week later

- can't pick up visual cues in interactions with people and so has trouble with how to behave socially

- has trouble with motor skills, sports, assembling puzzles

Causes of Learning Disabilities

Learning disabilities (LD's) and non-verbal learning disabilities (NLD's) are not caused by bad parenting, poor teaching, or cultural differences, as far as we know. They are due to organic, physiological, neurological causes. All of the brain mechanisms are present and in operating condition, but some of the 'wiring' does not work in the normal way. Advances in neuropsychology and neurophysiology will tell us more in the future. In some cases brain or nervous system development during pregnancy may be the problem. Causes may include maternal malnutrition, infectious disease, alcoholism; or birth problems (cord around the neck, breech delivery, long or difficult delivery depriving the brain of oxygen). Other disabilities can develop after birth, caused by fevers, blows, accidents, meningitis, drugs. Heredity can sometimes be a factor. There are many possible causes of learning disability, of the maturational lag, the neurological immaturity that causes LD, NLD, ADHD, and ADD.

The Brain

The brain is still a mystery. Scientists examining the causes of learning disabilities are learning more about the brain's composition. The organ is made of millions of nerve cells that have to communicate with other specific cells. The brain is the primary center for regulating and coordinating bodily activities. This great network of neurons (nerve cells) is divided into specialized areas: the hindbrain, the oldest, most primitive part of the brain includes the cerebellum which modulates skeletal muscles; the midbrain, or old mammalian brain, which aids in sensory and motor functions and connects the cerebellum with the hemispheres of the cerebrum; and the forebrain, including the cerebrum, the cerebral cortex.

The cerebrum represents about 85% of the weight of the brain. It is the largest, most advanced area and controls motor functions, sensory perception, speech, memory, emotions.

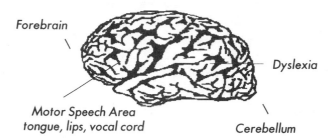

LEFT BRAIN

Forebrain

Dyslexia

*Motor Speech Area
tongue, lips, vocal cord*

Cerebellum

The cerebral cortex is organized into two halves, the right and left hemispheres. The left hemisphere contains areas specializing in the production of language and logic, the right hemisphere specializes in visual perception, music, emotions, and instinctive and nonverbal responses. The two areas must cooperate with motor and sensory areas of the cortex to create intelligent speech and written language or mathematics.

It is generally understood that LD is due to impairments or disorders in the left brain, and NLD is due to impairments of the right brain. The disabilities are the result of these neurological disorders.

Scientists are currently mapping the electrical activity of the brain, testing for deficiencies in certain neurotransmitters (the chemicals that transmit messages from one nerve cell to another), and investigating whatever other kinds of glitches they can discover in the complicated computer circuitry of the brain. Among the discoveries they have already made is that the inability to concentrate and pay attention that is one of the central factors in dyslexia and ADHD may be caused by a deficiency in specific neurotransmitters in specific areas of the brain. And the biologists are already discovering that there may be genetic factors that cause learning problems.

WHAT IS ATTENTION DEFICIT HYPERACTIVITY DISORDER (ADHD) OR ATTENTION DEFICIT DISORDER (ADD)?

It is important to remember that not all people with ADD or ADHD have learning disabilities. The literature suggests about 50%. And not all learning disabled people have the symptoms of ADD or ADHD. To repeat, the 'H' is the hyperactivity factor. It is possible to have all the complications of this disorder without the hyperactivity.

Sally Smith, author of *No Easy Answers* and founder of The Lab School of Washington, reports that 20 to 30 percent of people with attention deficit disorder are not hyperactive, and are actually hypoactive daydreamers with poor memory and social reticence. Dr. Edward Hallowell, author of *Driven to Distraction*, doesn't like the term at all. He says the whole label is incorrect, that the syndrome is not one of attention deficit, but of attention inconsistency and that most with ADD can actually focus intently when the subject is intensely interesting. He also objects to the word 'disorder' as it suggests pathology or illness, whereas there are in fact healthy advantages to having ADD, such as high energy, intuitiveness, creativity, and enthusiasm.

With these considerations duly noted, here is a list of symptoms of ADD or ADHD. (It must be stressed that the diagnosis of ADHD can only be made by a medical doctor or psychologist who sees the adult or child.)

DSM-IV says: "The essential feature of Attention-Deficit/Hyperactivity Disorder is a persistent pattern of inattention and/or hyperactivity-impulsivity that is more frequent and severe than is typically observed in individuals at a comparable level of development."

In short, ADD is a neurological problem whose main symptoms are: impulsivity; distractibility; excess energy. About 15 million Americans have ADHD or ADD, and many don't even know it.

DIAGNOSTIC CRITERIA IN CHILDREN (onset before age 7)
1. they fidget and squirm (in adolescents and adults it may be restless feelings)
2. they are easily distracted by external stimuli
3. it is hard for them to wait for turns, not to blurt out answers
4. there is difficulty following through on instructions
5. they have difficulty sustaining attention, staying on-task
6. they shift from one uncompleted activity to another
7. they talk excessively, interrupt, intrude on others
8. they do not seem to listen to what is being said
9. they often lose things necessary for tasks
10. they often engage in physically dangerous activities without considering consequences

DIAGNOSTIC CRITERIA FOR ADULTS
1. there is a sense of underachievement regardless of actual accomplishments
2. they have difficulty with organization
3. they often have trouble getting started, procrastination
4. there are too many projects, too little follow-through
5. they may clown, saying whatever comes to mind regardless of appropriateness
6. they have a need for stimulation, intensity, low tolerance for frustration, boredom

7.   they are easily distracted; they have trouble focusing; they tune out of conversations (unless personally interesting, and then they can hyperfocus without letup)
8.   they often possess highly intelligent creativity
9.   there is dislike of proper form, traditional procedure
10.   they are impulsive, impatient, hot-tempered, with a disregard for consequences
11.   they often change careers, relationships, plans abruptly
12.   they tend to be insecure, to worry

People who have ADHD may not have all the above symptoms, but they tend to have most of them significantly more often and with more intensity than people who do not have ADHD.

OTHER DISORDERS

There are other conditions that may accompany, hide, or resemble ADHD, such as anxiety disorder, depression, impulse-control disorders, obsessive-compulsive disorders, seizures, substance abuse. In addition, there are tic disorders such as Tourette's syndrome, personality disorders encompassing antisocial, borderline, and passive-aggressive disorders, pervasive development disorder, and psychotic disorders such as schizophrenia. A last example is autism, an impairment that may be associated with high-functioning intelligence as well as mental retardation, but is characterized by mental aloneness, undeveloped skills in social interaction and communication, an obsessive focus, and problems in the regulation of sensory intake and output (a hypersensitivity to whatever is seen and heard and felt). All of the above can hide or be confused with ADD or ADHD by a nonprofessional.

It is imperative, therefore, that proper diagnoses be made by licensed professionals.

2

THEIR FEELINGS AND REACTIONS,
YOUR FEELINGS AND REACTIONS

At the grocery store with ADD

- Your wife goes to the supermarket for the week's bulk grocery shopping, and comes home with winter mittens and three boxes of cereal, in tears. She complains once more of being too overwhelmed by too many choices in the store and too much chaos in her head. Once again, you are late for your boss's dinner party because she cannot get organized enough to get out of the house.

- Your son, star of the hockey team, and beloved for his pranks by friends, is a disaster in class. He can't sit still. He can't pay attention. He forgets what little he hears, and doesn't pass tests. His outlandish behavior has a purpose, aside from making his friends laugh; it's so that he gets kicked out of class in order to avoid classwork he can't do. This creates such terrible guilt in both parents and teachers who blame themselves for not being able to help him, they are ready to throw him at a wall or disown him.

- Your husband never seems to listen to what you are saying, interrupts intimacies with an inappropriate joke, makes sudden disappearances from a movie or family conversation, a chore or a game, changes jobs, careers, projects with a surprising abruptness considering his previous energetic intensity and your repeated remonstrations about his risk-taking. Without routine and structure, he grows anxious and moody. But he is so independent and restless, you don't want to risk his baleful glare by offering suggestions or direction.

- Your friend is a writer, an accomplished novelist published many times over. She is perfectly self-possessed giving a lecture, being interviewed on television or radio, holding affectionate interest and attention during a conversation with a loved person or two. But take her to a cocktail party or out to dinner with your friends where she is unrehearsed or with whom she is unfamiliar, and bright as she is, she seems totally incapable of picking up nonverbal social cues about how to behave. She is very capable of embarrassing you, your friends, herself, without even being aware of it.

LIVING WITH LEARNING DISABILITIES

It is all very well to recognize and understand the causes of ADD, ADHD, LD, NLD.

But behaviors cause feelings; actions cause reactions. On both sides, on the part of the person who has learning disabilities and on the part of those who love them and are affected, there is denial, frustration, anxiety, depression, guilt, despair. And anger most of all. Anger at the impairment, anger at the behavior and feelings caused by the disorder, both on the part of the person who has it, and the people affected, such as loved ones, friends, employers, teachers, and perhaps parents and spouses most of all.

THEIR FEELINGS AND REACTIONS TO THEIR BEHAVIORS

Children, adolescents, and adults with these subtle, invisible, neurological disabilities have enough problems with organization and memory, reading and writing or math skills. But these same disabilities, with or without the distractibility, impulsivity, or hyperactivity of ADHD, can interfere with normal social and emotional development and cause emotional and social stress. Learning disabled youngsters learn in their most impressionable years that they cannot perform, cannot understand the things other children do, and may grow into adults who have the feeling they're no good, they can't do anything right, and the whole world is nagging them. No matter if they have a special talent for sports or the arts or for popularity, there is always the gnawing feeling there's something wrong with them.

1. **resentment** (I see the world the only way I can and I'm met with ridicule, rejection, unkindness)

2. **self-hate** (constant failure doesn't leave me with very good feelings about myself)

3. **confusion** (I have only had this one brain all my life— it's hard to understand that it's different from other brains)

21

4. **frustration** (at being yelled at for being disorganized, forgetful, for not paying attention, not trying hard enough at school, at home, at work)

5. **bewilderment** (to constantly feel picked on for not doing anything right is to feel bewildered all the time)

6. **hopelessness** (I try my best, but I can't manage to achieve what others do)

7. **guilt** (am I worthless? bad? is it my fault?)

8. **rage** (why did I have to get stuck with this? and if I am stuck with this, why does everybody have to correct and criticize me all the time?)

9. **fear** (am I too dumb or crazy to bother with? am I always going to feel alone?)

10. **low self-esteem** (I cause too much trouble, I feel like an outcast, a misfit)

11. **anxiety** (I can't help worrying all the time. I always feel on the brink of failure, of going mad, of giving up because so much is so hard)

To suspect you are too stupid to get it, whatever it is you're supposed to get, to be put in special educational programs or demoted on the job or unable to cope with filling out forms, daily reading and writing, cleaning up your room or the garage, to have trouble finishing a project, dealing with ordinary social situations, never getting chosen for a team because of your lack of motor skills or because you get short-circuited with too much coming at you at once — all these difficulties that other people don't seem to have to deal with, make someone with learning disabilities feel different, separate, a failure, distrustful, a social alien, unlike anyone else.

Human beings are a herd species. People with learning disabilities feel left out of the herd, unacceptable among their own kind, ridiculed for being stupid or crazy. They learn to blame and hate themselves and can feel suicidally alone and depressed. This is especially true for those with allied neurological problems like sensory integrative disorders or autism, people so sensitive to touch they cannot even be reassured by a hug.

Even when the disabilities are diagnosed there still remains the problem of lifelong management: behavior modifications; adaptive or compensation techniques; perhaps a lifelong need for medication. And there is the constant reminder, from the puzzled expression on the faces of others, that the disability makes the person who has it different and others uncomfortable or annoyed.

YOUR FEELINGS AND REACTIONS TO THEIR BEHAVIORS

1. **frustration** (you can understand this thing till you turn blue, you can develop a sense of humor, help them to make lists, provide structure and organization, limit directions and criticisms, bite your tongue while their rooms and closets are a mess, their memories and handwriting are chaos, and you still have to face a waterfall of tantrums or a wall of charm as your loved one tries to escape the grueling difficulties of routine or responsibilities so difficult for them to handle)

2. **disappointment** (when your wife takes yet another risk with the grocery money; your son dedicates himself yet again to a collision course with the wrong people, drugs, the police; your manic friend who cannot live without the constant stimulation of center stage yet again dances on the table at your dinner party)

23

3. **anger** (I have to take on too many responsibilities because my husband forgets or can't remember things that have to be done)

4. **embarrassment** (my wife has no social judgment, and I always worry or have to cover for her embarrassing remarks and behavior)

5. **rejection** (I feel so rejected by my son's rage when I try to help)

6. **annoyance** (learning disabled people often develop at an early age the survival strategies and charm, the avoidance and denial of the best of cons. It helps them get through situations when they don't know what to do. These techniques may help them feel better. They may help you feel anything from annoyed to homicidal)

7. **guilt** (no matter how often the psychologist reminds you that your loved one's neurological problems are not your fault, your brain plays tapes that begin with, "If only I had — or had not....")

8. **remorse** (more "If only I had said or done or been....")

9. **fear** (that the loved one's life will get worse — and yours along with it)

10. **hurt** (when your child is called 'retard' or 'spaz' or 'dumbhead' you are hurt, too, because your child has been hurt, because you've all tried so hard, because he really can't button and zip, write, finish the work, pay attention, get along with the others)

11. **confusion** (I can't figure out how her head works, I don't understand why he can't tell me how he feels, I

don't see why he can't learn, can't listen to me, she makes the same mistakes over and over and over, why his distractibility makes him like a bull in a china shop)

12. **blamed and attacked** (families and friends are often thrown by being accused of causing the problems, and we get tired of explaining and defending)

13. **superiority** (I feel better than my friend)

14. **desire to avoid** (I'm tired of all this trouble and confusion, even my loved one's enthusiasm and energy)

15. **compassion** (it must be so hard to be them, after all, they try so hard; a true affection)

All these feelings are more or less acute, depending on how dependent you are on someone else's behavior. An excellent thing to examine, actually, is whether or not we are too dependent on someone else's behavior. You can also try to remember why you fell in love with your sweetheart, how adorable your difficult child was when he pointed out the moon, how enthusiastically your friend supports your life.

But as you contemplate life or friendship, being child or parent, spouse or friend to a person with learning disabilities, you might think about others who have had them.

Remarkable People with Learning Disabilities

Einstein

Hans Christian Andersen

Mozart

- Albert Einstein, the scientist who revolutionized our understanding of time, space, the universe, the laws of physics was found by his teachers to be a slow learner, especially in reading, and he was socially awkward his whole life.

- Auguste Rodin, sculptor, was so slow reading and writing, he was the worst student in his school.

- Mozart, among the most brilliant composers who ever lived, did not speak until he was four years old.

- Hans Christian Andersen, writer of the fairy tales on which Disney depends, was immature, socially difficult, a terrible student, disorderly, and disruptive.

Others with learning disabilities include politician and statesman Winston Churchill, inventor Thomas Edison, the great American poet Walt Whitman, artist and general genius Leonardo da Vinci, thriller-writer Agatha Christie.

There have been U.S. presidents, great athletes, doctors, and lawyers, as well as artists and scientists, who are and have been learning disabled. Because they are not influenced and controlled by their culture in the usual fashion, often people with learning disabilities see the world in new, fresh ways. And because they cannot function in the usual manner, their focus or their escape may be to concentrate and strengthen their unique and particular talents. You may, in knowing someone with learning disabilities, be in touch not just with a collection of disabilities, but with one of nature's miracles.

3

MANNERS AND COPING AIDS: BOTH SIDES

Learning disabilities can threaten all sorts of relationships: boss and employee; husband and wife; parent and child; siblings; teacher and student; friends. There are manners, and coping aids, for both sides, that can help.

Begin with the courtesy of remembering that the problem is *physical* not *willful*, a *neurological* not a *moral* issue. Good will on both sides helps. So does a sense of humor. Know that there are resources to improve the whole situation.

The objectives are to maximize good communication, and to minimize the power struggle.

TIPS FOR YOU

1. Know what you are dealing with. Seek an accurate diagnosis (see Chapter Five), so you know you are dealing with LD, or NLD, ADD, or ADHD, and not just anxiety or too much coffee or a sociopath.

2. Respect and affection work better than resentment.

3. A sense of humor is essential. Life with someone who dances to a different beat can be funny sometimes, provide a fresh point of view at others. When you have a choice between murder or laughter, go for the laugh.

4. Technical help is relatively easy to get. This is true whether it is in the form of special teachers to acquire skills in school or in the workplace; or psychologists to suggest skills in living. But your relationship will best survive with mutual help. TALK TO EACH OTHER — about your feelings, fears, resentments, hopes, interests, dreams, disappointments.

5. Do plan treatment. The problem is **physical**. The problem is **real**. The problem needs **help**. Whether that help is special education, appropriate psychotherapy, or medication is up to your specialists and you.

6. Two daily tips: **Make lists** — from home chores to car directions to the day's activities; from the names of your children to grocery necessities; from what you need to what the baby needs. Leave pads and pencils everywhere, especially by the telephone. **Break big tasks down into smaller segments**: one part of any activity at a time—you can build a house one brick at a time.

7. Do not role-play and set the roles in cement: I know, you don't know; pesterer and pest; I'm the regular human being, you're from Mars.

8. Don't do controller and controlled. Power struggles are a waste of energy, and nobody ever wins.

9. Try not to do verbal attacks, or criticize too much. The tapes in the heads of people who have neurological disabilities are already brutal enough.

10. *Do praise* instead, for whatever is well done.

11. *Do capitalize* on each other's strengths. If you organize best, do that. Let your friend supply the enthusiasm and energy and appreciation, the stamina, the good will.

12. Try to empathize. Make a daily decision whether you want to be helpful or destructive to your LD friend and your relationship. Your new understanding of the problem can be used as a weapon or a way to find solutions.

13. If you don't understand the way the other head is working, ask questions. Curiosity can be very informative.

TIPS FOR THEM

1. Find professional help. Not only is an accurate diagnosis necessary, but detailed explanations of the behaviors and feelings and difficulties in their neurological conditions.

2. Be aware of the difficulties imposed on loved ones. If it's hard to remember a birthday or a friend arriving on an airplane, or to focus in on a desperate spouse trying to communicate something, or to restrain an impulse to go to the movies or Chicago instead of feeding the children, or even to think before speaking, or reflect before acting — it is hardly surprising that just because there is finally a diagnosis of LD, NLD, ADD, or ADHD, all the anger, resentment, guilt, and frustration doesn't go away. BE PATIENT.

3. SEEK TREATMENT. A diagnosis is an explanation, not an excuse to go on with the old behaviors.

4. Let them BE RESPONSIBLE FOR THEMSELVES. Do as much as possible on their own. They can ask for help with those things that are difficult to do or cope with.

5. Learn self-advocacy with others. Don't expect college staff, employers, spouses, friends, to guess what they need. They must learn to explain whatever learning difficulties they have.

6. Learn self-advocacy with themselves. Remind themselves they are not lazy, too stupid to plan or focus on something, bad because they lack perception of the environment around them, because they don't always get it, whatever *it* is.

7. Learn not to use their disabilities as an excuse for bad manners. They may have learning problems, they may have low tolerance for frustration. It's easy to explode. Better to talk it out instead of letting the pot boil over.

8. When all else fails, remember it is possible to start life over every five minutes.

9. Make notes and lists. Wear pencil and paper around the neck, if necessary.

10. Never be afraid of making mistakes. Nobody ever learned much from success.

4

SEEKING DIAGNOSIS

The field of learning disabilities is a new one. Until this century, learning disabilities were confused with mental retardation or mental illness. This confusion still goes on.

1. To treat any problem properly, it is imperative to have the correct diagnosis. No one would treat a broken leg with an arm sling. No one should treat learning disabled people as if they required electroconvulsive shock therapy.

2. Today neuroscientists have a better understanding of memory and learning, and better tools to examine the brain than even twenty years ago. Because of this, parents are less resistant to having their children examined (and a learning-disability diagnosis qualifies a student for extra help). Spouses who know their partners are smart even if they can't spell, or their attention span doesn't outlast soft-boiling an egg, are seeking diagnoses (helpful living-with-LD-ADD tools are out there). While research neurobiologists investigate the cause, we are concerned here with the nature of the problem (the diagnosis), and what to do about it (the treatment).

DIAGNOSIS AND EVALUATION

The process of diagnosis and evaluation of a learning disability is not as easy as diagnosing an X-ray. Learning experts depend on several factors.

1. classroom or life experience observations

2. family interviews

3. a medical report

4. psychological evaluation, intelligence and achievement tests, neurological screening

Don't be discouraged. Your own therapist, your family doctor, your school or college, a local university, will refer you to a qualified psychologist. This psychologist will be certified to do the psychological testing, the coordinating of all the other tests, reports, and interviews, the final evaluation, neurological screening, personality assessment, and diagnostic summary. This psychologist will also provide recommendations for treatment that may include only special education assistance or special skills assistance; therapy; perhaps the kind of medication that allays anxiety and helps to focus; medication for the depression caused by the learning disability; or any combination of the above.

The psychologist you are referred to for tests and diagnosis should be certified to do the testing.

THE TESTS

There are hundreds of tests that measure aptitude, achievement, vocational interests, hearing and visual perception, mental health, and motor skills. There are many tests that measure only I.Q. — intelligence. The Wechsler tests, designed by American psychologist David Wechsler, are the most commonly administered. Wechsler defined intelligence as "the overall capacity of an individual to understand and cope with the world." The Wechsler Intelligence Scale for Children-Revised (WISC-R) is used for children ages 6-16. The Wechsler Adult Intelligence Test-Revised (WAIS-R) is given to individuals age 16 and up.

What Wechsler understood was that the right brain and the left brain each specializes in a different way of thinking and learning. He found a way to test both the left brain (verbal information) and the right brain (visual comprehension and imagination). His exam contains both verbal scales and performance scales. The results can be averaged together to obtain an intelligence quotient (I.Q.). The results can also display the **discrepancies** that indicate learning disabilities.

(One of the authors of this book had an off-the-charts verbal score, and a pretty low visual-spacial score — a clear indication of NLD. To this day, she suffers from a lack of social judgment, an inability to finish copying a five-minute block design in under an hour, and a generally iffy right brain.)

The more serious the disability, the more tests are usually given. Other tests are:

- Wide Range Achievement Test (WRAT)

- Wechsler Individual Achievement Test (WIAT)

- Spache Oral Diagnostic Reading Test

- Marianne Frostig Development Test of Visual Perception

- Detroit Test of Learning Aptitude

- Thematic Apperception Test (TAT)

- Rorschach Inkblot Test (personality assessment)

- Bender Gestalt (for neuropsychological screening)

In addition to the above, a medical examination is necessary to rule out impairments of vision, hearing, problems with speech such as stuttering, or malnutrition as the source of the learning disabilities. And a further psychological evaluation may be necessary to rule out other problems, other disorders. Environmental causes such as alcohol abuse, physical abuse, and so forth need to be ruled out, too.

The earlier in someone's life these tests and evaluations are made, the better the prospects of coping well with learning disabilities and the fewer the scars left from wounds to the psyche.

TREATMENTS

No one treatment is absolute. Learning disability is a matter of degree as well as type, and the people who have learning disabilities are all different in terms of intelligence, talents and skills, emotional stability, and personality development.

- Special education assistance, special skills tutoring at school or at work, special adaptive aids (computers that check spelling, have templates that make it easier to write letters and fill out forms; answering machines to make for more accurate telephone messages; how-to-videos to learn from instead of books, and so forth)

- Skills therapy from a psychologist: social skills training therapy; help in dealing with low self-worth; help with impulse control, focusing attention, more effective planning and scheduling

- Behavior modification: further tools for living that can include asking a friend or family member to be a coach and aid in listing the day's activities, keeping a calendar of the month's events, going over school or business conference reports, helping with any other general organizational problem or needs for structure

- Psychotherapy for mood management, environmental improvement, relationship problems, scars from the past, present resentments

- Medication

There are two main classes of drugs used for people with learning disabilities and especially attention deficit disorders with or without hyperactivity. They are stimulants and antidepressants. The use of drugs has undoubtedly helped both children and adults, along with educational support and psychotherapy, to calm and focus the attention, reduce unfocused hyperactivity, reduce anxiety, impulsivity, and frustration, irritability, and mood swings. The drugs help to increase efficiency because they foster an increased ability to concentrate, to think clearly, and to stay on task. Of course, drugs must be monitored, doses adjusted, and side effects carefully watched by a medically qualified doctor.

Ritalin is the stimulant most often used in adults and children for ADHD. There has recently been fierce controversy over the use of Ritalin in children. Some of the reasons are: an inappropriate use of the drug for what are merely discipline problems in energetic children; lack of supervision of side effects; a too liberal dosage; a general distaste for drugging children rather than changing our educational system to accommodate individual learning needs. Yet Ritalin's effectiveness in helping both children and adults to control hyperactivity, improve focus, work better, organize better, and be more generally productive and content with their lives and themselves, is evident.

Antidepressants such as Norpramin, the tricyclic Tofranil, the newer drugs such as Wellbutrin also seem to help people with problems in focusing. Prozac is sometimes used for the depression component, Zoloft for anxiety. There are other and will be even newer drugs, of course, but it is well to remember that because learning disabilities are *physical* problems, a physical treatment such as an appropriate drug may be part, though never all, of the solution.

COPING

The causes of learning disabilities are fascinating, but what matters most to the friends and families, and naturally even more to the learning disabled people themselves, is treatment and all the various ways to cope.

For younger children, coping means learning skills that enable them to read and keep up with their classmates, so they don't feel bad about themselves or scared about being left out of the herd.

For adolescents and young adults, coping may mean finding special schools or colleges capable of special educational classes and assistance. It is with adolescence that social perception learning disabilities begin to announce themselves most clearly. There are not only the usual problems of adolescence (independence fighting with continuing dependencies; the surge of

*You get left out —
the lion gets you.*

36

hormones; cultural expectations and the terrors of failure; drugs; crime). If there is NLD, there may be extra social disabilities that label a person an outcast, a nerd, a geek, someone just too different to belong anywhere.

For adults as well as children, coping means:

1. balancing independence with aid given by a family coach, a support group, a therapist, a teacher

2. suggesting the kind of work that is based on skills, not confounded by disabilities (conventional careers are often not the answer)

3. educating yourself and others that the problem is rooted in biology, not weakness of character

4. structuring daily chores and schedules with lists, notes to the self, reminders, files, written schedules

5. acknowledging the need for intensity by embracing healthy challenges, staying busy (intensity wards off chaos, depression)

6. making allowances for quirky behavior if it works — paying bills in front of the TV, doing homework in a treehouse, breaking down large tasks into smaller components with time out in between the segments

7. dealing with mood management — LD people are moody, and if changing an activity (from reading to taking a walk, for instance) or naming the feeling (this lessens confusion and frustration) don't help, remember the mood will pass anyway

8. doing a lot of physical exercise — lessens anxiety, frustration, expands the mind, cheers the soul

9. making good use of people — it is important to pick supportive friends, seek involved teachers, understanding bosses, and above all, a cheerful, positive, independent mate in life

10. staying socially connected by organizing social dates and calendars, scheduling activities with friends, in order not to become isolated

Suggested Teaching Aids

Both children and adults who have LD, NLD, ADHD, and who are in the process of education, will benefit from:

- highly structured classrooms

- easy, clear assignments with flexibility

- untimed tests to minimize anxiety and maximize the point, which is to learn, not just perform

- special classes and tutoring

- close partnership between special-education teachers, tutors, and classroom teachers

- individualized education plan, ungraded system based on individual goals

- relaxed, positive atmosphere

Actually, this sounds ideal for everyone.

5

LIVING WITH LD, NLD, ADD, ADHD
LIFE STORIES

TOM

As a boy, Tom was everyone's favorite — and everyone's nightmare. He fidgeted and squirmed. He could not pay attention, finish a task, clean up anything, organize himself or his work. He clowned, ran off, threw spitballs or temper tantrums. He made trouble everywhere.

But he was charming and affectionate as well, and most found it difficult to discipline him. It was strange that his parents, whose careers were in medicine and mental health, never noticed Tom's problems. And his teachers never made a point of reporting the problems Tom was having with schoolwork, but slid him on from grade to grade.

For one thing, he was well-mannered, adorable, and polite. For another, he was a particularly gifted athlete, popular, and with his good manners and good humor, an asset to the spirit of the classroom. As he grew older, his outstanding abilities in basketball, track, baseball, and especially as a football running back, made the whole school proud. His teachers simply passed him from grade to grade, with comments about his being a late bloomer, and added that his leadership and his sense of responsibility for others on the playing fields made him a pleasure and an asset to the whole school.

They all knew what Tom knew: that he could not retain what he knew long enough to pass a simple test (unless it was the random luck of multiple choice tests); that among other severe language difficulties, the confusion in organizing what he heard was reflected in his confused speech patterns; that he was so distracted in class, he could not finish what he started, or organize his material. He had trouble following directions, and he lost everything from his notes to his pencil.

He was graduated from high school with the help of the smart girlfriends he was always careful to choose. He got into college on the strength of his football talent. And he chose the restaurant business as a career because it allowed him to do something physical rather than intellectual and to use his charm and his people skills. He chose partners and management to fill in the gaps in his capabilities — very intelligent life choices.

Nobody had ever tested Tom. His is the story of a learning disabled child, adolescent, and young man whose wide discrepancies in ability were overlooked, who got through because he hid his disabilities behind his abilities.

What he also hid successfully for years into his adulthood were his feelings about himself: that he was stupid, crazy, or both, because after all, he was painfully aware of his history of reading difficulties, his distraction problems, his impulsivity, his differentness from his friends. His anxiety at being found wanting and his fear of subsequent rejection or sudden failure grew. In his early forties, both his marriage and his restaurant interests fell apart.

His wife punished him verbally and constantly for risk-taking and for what she called his obsessive behavior, whether it was golf (the successor to football), or for working too many hours at the restaurant, for forgetting their appointments or to finish raking the leaves. His restaurant interests fell apart for him because, like many learning disabled people, he was a trusting person, and had for once trusted the wrong friend.

It was suggested that Tom be tested. The results were that he had ADD, and left brain learning disabilities that involved language skills. When Tom, an extremely intelligent man, finally understood — with the help of both psychotherapy and medication to slow the chaos down so he could see his life frame by frame instead of in the customary confusing jumble of fast motion — he was able to sort things out.

Eventually, he began a new business, also making use of his considerable physical abilities, and, after a divorce, a new marriage with someone who celebrated his talents rather than denigrated his disabilities, and who enjoyed his fun.

A sense of fun

DANA

As a child, she was pretty, graceful, and so full of openly expressed individuality and intense energy, she exhausted and annoyed her mother. In reaction, Dana became rebellious and often rude. But she was so verbally bright, she eventually interested her father, an intellectual and a surgeon. He brought her up as he would a son, encouraging in her both athletic and professional performance. He neither noticed nor cared about the lack of social skills that so distressed her mother.

Dana did brilliantly in all verbal schoolwork, especially in writing skills, and if she couldn't do anything that involved spacial relationships, wrote stories to shine for her teachers. Her math skills were lacking, but no one cared because she was a girl.

The father blamed the child's eventual sullen depressions on the mother's rejection of her. The teachers and the mother blamed the father's preoccupation with his own career for his child's stiff isolation from her classmates, her daydreaming, her now withdrawn intensity. Everyone blamed Dana herself for the fierce rebellions of her childhood and adolescence.

As an adult, her life has read like a romantic adventure novel. She was disinherited and reinherited regularly by an appalled mother. While in college, she eloped with her high school sweetheart, ran off to live in Japan with him for a year, returned to bear two children, publish the first four of her books, divorce, and remarry, all before her thirtieth birthday. In the next twelve years, she became a prize-winning author of over forty books, married and divorced again, and bloomed into a miserable, confused, hard-drinking alcoholic.

She went to A.A., recovered, published more books, married a fourth time, divorced a fourth time, and spent her early fifties beginning a new life, outside of New York City where she had grown up, on a salt marsh in Connecticut. Now she traveled the world, taught in India each winter for several years, learned and was licensed to rehabilitate wildlife. At 59, she started a small publishing house, and, after many years on her own, fell deeply in love.

Curious about the endless pattern of reinventing herself and her life over and over again, and about her ongoing 'people problems' as she referred to them (her inability to read people on the spot much of the time, though she could analyze and write about them afterwards), her exhaustion after a few hours of being with anyone, her lack of social eptness or capacity for judging what to say to whom and when, and the combination of her passionate caring for what happened to the human race coupled with her inability to stand being with most of them for more than an hour — she had herself tested.

Dana had NLD — a nonverbal learning disability, a right-brain impairment. Her verbal pyrotechnics had hidden her inability to relate properly to people, to pick up the normal cues that enable someone to be appropriately intimate with a mate. Her caring and affection, her verbal and analytical skills had compensated. But she always knew her behavior with people was different, had always assumed she was crazy, and had retreated into her books, her children, a few close friends, and a kind of inner isolation despite her worldwide acquaintance.

The diagnosis and the therapy that helped Dana understand the problem and learn to practice new social skills, freed Dana from old behaviors and feelings and allowed her to move among her own species with less terror and far more pleasure.

JEREMY

The two homes Jeremy has lived in all his life have been war zones: his parents' home while he was growing up; and his own home now, shared with his wife and two sons.

Growing up in his parents' home was a nightmare of attack and defense:

43

"What do you mean, he failed again?" Jeremy can still hear his father's roar. "Why can't he pass a single, bloody test? He's a screw-up, that's why. I didn't think he was stupid. Maybe I was wrong. He's a stupid screw-up."

"He's promised to get help." Jeremy can also hear his mother's begging voice.

"He's promised before. He never shows up. He never keeps a promise. I'll bet he's running around with those outlaws he calls his friends again."

"Why are we always fighting about Jeremy — is he all you care about?" Jeremy can still hear also the resentful protests of his younger brother, who hated all the attention Jeremy got, even if it was negative.

Now in his own home with his own family, Jeremy is still living the same nightmare:

"Can't you be on time just once when we're expected at my mother's for dinner? And I suppose you forgot to pick up the cake for dessert. You can remember a bowling date all right."

"What do you mean, you bought into Jack's garage? That's twice you've gambled our IRA's on one of Jack's risky businesses. I keep talking about responsibility, and you keep taking risks. Can't you just keep a normal job like everyone else?"

"Ma, could you stop yelling at daddy all the time?"

"Dad — how come you didn't show at Father's Day at school?"

Jeremy has spent a lifetime running away. He runs because he can't read or spell properly. He runs because he has such a low threshold of boredom and frustration, because it's so hard to focus for long. He runs because he can't help forgetting things and knows it; he runs because he has little control over his impulses. He runs because he knows he takes business risks, so he

44

can work for himself, so he never has to lose another job because he can't follow directions properly. He runs because he can't stand bringing misery everywhere he lives, to everyone he loves. He runs because he can't stand himself, or any more failure. He runs because he feels dumb. Because he feels nuts. He runs because he can't stand still.

CHRIS

Mother: "My son is not a problem. My son is who he is."

Teacher: "He can't stop moving. He distracts the other children. We've had to put him at a desk by himself at the back of the room."

Mother: "Okay. So he sits by himself. Doesn't mean the other kids don't like him. He's popular with everyone."

Teacher: "Yes, he is. But he'd be so much better off on Ritalin."

Mother: "You mean he'd be easier for you to manage. I don't want my son on drugs. I'd rather teach him how to control his own hyperactivity. He's smart enough."

Teacher: "Yes. He's smart enough. But he'd learn so much more easily if he could concentrate better."

Mother: "Learn what? That he's not okay the way he is? Not on your life."

Besides the psychological effect of being on a drug, the mother had also investigated some of the physical side effects that were possible, including addiction. She agreed to reevaluate when Chris was older, if his life became too difficult without medical intervention.

JANE

College professor: "She's quiet and polite. She smiles nicely as if she's understood every word I've said. She just doesn't learn anything. Or learns something partially. Or forgets it immediately she's learned it."

Mother: "I know. It's been the same all her life. She can't even remember a movie we've gone to. She can sit through it all again, and not know she's seen it before."

Father: "And she's as absent-minded as an old professor — excuse the reference. They say Einstein forgot, and wore house slippers with his dinner clothes when he went out in the evening. That's what Jane is like. Her mind's on her art or nothing at all."

College psychologist: "Funny you should compare Jane to Einstein — he had a learning disability, too."

Father: "Well, she's no Einstein — can't even read too well. All she seems to do is draw — and draw, and draw, and draw."

There are two simple things to say about Jane. She has an auditory perception disability. And she is a gifted child with an exceptional talent in art.

The auditory perception disability interferes with learning. Her brain has problems discriminating sounds (although her hearing is perfect); it has problems with memory, sequential memory, understanding. Reading, for instance, is a visual-auditory association. Since perception, the sorting out of information, is the foundation on which all learning is based, Jane is in trouble. Her brain has trouble discriminating between two sounds, or distinguishing the important sound from all the background sounds. This is troubling whether she is in a movie, trying to pay attention in class, trying to follow directions, take a telephone message, or remember what she is supposed to do next.

46

The biggest problem, as always, is everyone's reactions. Now she has come upon teachers who will individualize her education, give her vocational rehabilitation counseling, train her to compensate for her disability, and most of all, who will encourage her valuable attributes — her dependable dedication to her friends, her work, and to her craft.

Intelligent children who fail to learn, intelligent adults who fail to progress in ways society deems appropriate, thrive nicely with a little help in organizing the disorder, minimizing the frustration, and socialization skills. Above all, they thrive in an atmosphere where their energy and talents are appreciated. And the lack of discrimination that makes them treat everyone equally, the sheer joy and freshness of vision that accompany the lack of deadening memory, the delightful spontaneity that is often lost among normally maturing people, the wandering adventurousness of those who are more impulsive and less careful — these qualities in learning disabled people attract and draw other people to them.

And perhaps learning disabilities are the well from which spring much great art and science. The inability to be bored that may lead to intense absorption in a singular passion has given us Mozart's music, Einstein's physics, Andersen's fairy tales, and the light bulb!

6

RESOURCES: SPECIAL EDUCATION; IDEA AND ADA; SUPPORT SYSTEMS AND SERVICES

Sadly, many people with learning disabilities never find the help they need, never suspect there are tools they can use to allow them to cope. To become productive, to cooperate with and relate to others as friend, parent, mate, to feel part of instead of outside the universe to which we all belong — this has for so long been denied to those learning disabled people who cannot fit the system or pick up the usual clues for survival. They often fail, or else they are driven constantly to succeed, over and over again. As Dr. Kathleen Laundy, clinical instructor of the Yale Child Study Center says, "Children and adults with learning disabilities have lifelong challenges to show what they know to the world."

Sally Smith, founder of The Lab School in Washington, DC and author of *No Easy Answers* (focusing on children with LD at home and at school) and *Succeeding Against the Odds* (focuses on adults with LD), is a leading force in the field of learning disabilities. She not only advocates for the learning disabled person, but asks, "What about the devastation of the entire family unit when an intelligent young person with potential falls by the wayside because of lack of necessary support services?"

SPECIAL EDUCATION

The Lab School of Washington is a prototype education center for people with learning disabilities, although there are others now across the country as well. The Lab School has a day school full of intelligent, often gifted children from primary school 5-6-year-olds through teenagers in high school. It has a night school to help adults strengthen academic, communications, and employment skills, a clinic for testing and tutoring, and a full range of support services and products for teaching the learning disabled. The Lab School also has a summer program, an international outreach program, and a training center for those who wish to learn to teach. For more information: *Lab School of Washington, 4759 Reservoir Road NW, Washington, DC 20016, (202) 965-6600.*

Landmark, in Massachusetts, is the largest school in the country for dyslexic students. The Gow School, founded in 1926, is the nation's oldest school for dyslexic students. Adelphi University in New York has had a program for learning disabled students since 1979. There are schools, centers, organizations, colleges, universities all over the country dedicated to the support of learning disabled children and adults. Although some LD children, through neural maturation and systematic special education either grow out of or learn to compensate for their disabilities, most carry their difficult baggage through life. With experienced teaching and support services, many thrive well.

Here are several important organizations to contact. The addresses and telephone numbers of these and others are listed in the appendix.

- **Learning Disabilities Association of America**

- **National Center for Learning Disabilities**

- **National Information Center for Children and Youths with LD**

- **National Network of LD Adults**

- **Office of Vocational Rehabilitation Services**

- **C.H.A.D.D.** (Children with Attention Deficit Disorders)

- **Association on Handicapped Student Service Programs in Postsecondary Education** (AHSSPPEE)

- **AbleData** (maintains a computerized database of products for learning disabilities and other disabilities)

- **ERIC Clearinghouse on Disabilities and Gifted Education Council for Exceptional Children** (free publications)

- **A.D.D.A.** (Attention Deficit Disorder Association is a national alliance of support groups that provides referrals and information)

- **Peterson's Colleges with Programs for LD Students** (lists colleges)

- **Schoolsearch Guide to Colleges with Programs or Services for Students with LD**

Public Law 94-142: Education for All Handicapped Children Act

By law, a *free public education* is guaranteed to all between the ages of 3 and 21.

Each handicapped person is guaranteed an IEP, an individualized education program.

The law also itemizes other procedural safeguards that include training for special education teachers, testing, consultation with parents, employment support, and other related services.

IDEA (Individuals with Disabilities Education Act)

This is the new name for Public Law 94-142. The age range is more inclusive, and the term 'handicapped children' has been replaced with the now more preferred term 'children with disabilities.'

ADA (Americans with Disabilities Act)

In 1990, the ADA was signed into law. There are legal advocacy agencies that can help. For referral call the organizations listed above or in the appendix of this book. You can also call or write to the U.S. Department of Justice, Civil Rights Division. They are interested not only in architectural, but procedural compliance.

The ADA focuses on eliminating discrimination against individuals with disabilities and bringing them into the economic and social mainstream of American life. It emphasizes that there should be reasonable accommodations for an applicant or employee whose physical or mental limitations are known. This not only includes wider doorways and ramps for people in wheel-chairs, telecommunications devices for the deaf, services for people with visual impairments, but technology for those with learning disabilities. Spellcheck software in computers, answering machines, and other telecommunications devices are helpful examples.

Larry B. Silver, M.D., author of *The Misunderstood Child* and clinical professor of psychiatry at Georgetown University School of Medicine, is himself learning disabled. He tells a story at the end of his book, an excellent and much-praised guide for parents of children with learning disabilities. When he was acting director of the National Institute of Mental Health, attending a congressional budget hearing, some spelling errors were corrected on a note he wrote. As he said, everybody knows if you can't spell, you must be dumb!

Just another Einstein.

Just another Einstein.

7

OTHER CONDITIONS

There are other conditions, many previously mentioned, that create learning disabilities and cause the ADHD behaviors, hyperactivity, distractibility, impulsivity. Again, we are not discussing mental illness or mental retardation (although either may be present), but **organic**, **neurological**, **brain chemistry impairments** that interfere with ordinary learning.

Note: anxiety and depression may accompany any or all ADHD behaviors, any or all learning disabilities. Accurate diagnosis is essential to distinguish between emotional illness and brain impairments.

The following physical disorders interfere with learning to greater and lesser extents.

SENSORY DISORDERS
- Visual impairment and blindness
- Hearing impairment and deafness
- Lack of sensation, including lack of ability to feel touch, pain, or temperature changes

COMMUNICATION DISORDERS

Articulation, stammering or stuttering, language disorders caused by central nervous system defects that result in an inability to produce language (a sort of short-circuit in the system of sending and receiving messages)

AUTISM

Autism is the most widely recognized of the category of Pervasive Developmental Disorders. These are complex developmental disabilities in which there are severe impairments involving language and communication skills and social interactions. Pervasive Developmental Disorders include Rett syndrome, childhood disintegrative disorder, and Asperger syndrome.

People with autism may be high-functioning or low-functioning, possess extremely high I.Q.'s or be untestable. But all exhibit lifelong information processing problems in language, thinking, communications, and social relations. The processing of sensory information is often highly disturbed. This may result in so heightened a sensitivity, that touch, sound, and sight, especially light, may cause not only confusion but pain. Babies with autism may grow rigid and scream when they are held close and need to be fed propped up on a pillow.

Donna Williams, among the high-functioning adults with autism, describes in one of her two books *Somebody, Somewhere*, a state of language-meaning deafness and emotion-feeling blindness. Oliver Sachs, in his *Anthropologist from Mars*, describes an interview with Temple Grandon, also a high-functioning person with autism, a scientist and an innovator in humane cattle management, who speaks of love and true relationship to another human being wistfully, because she cannot feel it. One an author, one a scientist — they both have severe neurological problems, impairments in managing sensory stimulation and in processing the external world.

Others with autism may be less fortunate. Severe overreactions to the external world may include: screaming, tantrums, head-banging, tensing; self-biting or other self-mutilations; a general shutting out of the world of people, although objects may be normally enjoyed. Mental aloneness is the cardinal feature of autism, as is obsessive, repetitive, ritualistic insistence on sameness.

Strange to contemplate, but the obsessive focus on repetition can lead to exceptional memory and achievements, and, untouched by outside culture, unusual originality of thought and invention. This, in spite of the learning disabilities autism entails.

ANTISOCIAL PERSONALITY DISORDER

People with this disease have been referred to as psychopaths or sociopathic personalities. The DSM-IV diagnostic criteria for APD describes "a pervasive pattern of disregard for and violation of the rights of others...lying...conning...aggressiveness ...reckless disregard for others." They not only lack empathy, but are callous and contemptuous of the feelings, rights, and sufferings of others. The diagnosis of APD is made for people 18 years of age and over who have a childhood and/or adolescent pattern of Conduct Disorder. People with APD cannot learn from experience, and have too many attendant behaviors to profit from ordinary education.

These are the people who hurt and kill without remorse, Bundy, Manson, and the like. But they are also to be found in boardrooms and on the sports fields, among politicians (think of Hitler and Stalin), as well as in mobs, gangs, on the streets.

Most recent findings as to cause are based not only on abusive, unattached, unbonded childhoods, but on genetic (physical) aberrations. There is no cure for adult psychopaths.

OTHER GENETIC CONDITIONS

People with genetic conditions such as cerebral palsy, sei-
zure disorders, tic disorders such as Tourette's disorder may also
have learning disabilities or display ADHD behaviors — and *do
not* have mental illness or mental retardation any more often
than anybody else.

AND LAST — THE GIFTED CHILD

A gifted child, one with exceptional I.Q., talent, brilliance in
a particular field — the arts, science, sports, the performing arts
— is as unusual, special, and can be as difficult to educate and
understand neurologically as any other differently organized
person. Often, such people are gifted in many disciplines, not
just one. The Marland Report, presented by the U.S. Office of
Education in 1970, presented some interesting facts about gifted
and talented children in the U.S. Of the identified 1.5 to 2.5 mil-
lion gifted and talented children, adjustment problems were so great that they represented 3.4 percent of school dropouts. About half of the gifted children became 'mental dropouts' at around ten years of age. Either we bore them or put them on pedestals.

A gifted adult can be defined by tests — the top one percent level of I.Q. tests like the Stanford-Binet Intelligence Scale. Or giftedness can be recognized

*Pedestals are chilly—
and very, very lonely.*

in high performance. Howard Gardner believes there are seven intelligences: linguistic; musical; logical-mathematical; spatial; bodily-kinesthetic; interpersonal; intrapersonal (a talent for self-knowledge, introspection).

Talent needs encouragement, mentoring, and practice — it cannot develop without proper education, proper and constant exercise, proper nurturance. As the human race needs all the help it can get, we need to pay attention to those who can inspire or inch us forward.

THE HUMAN BRAIN ITSELF

The final condition for learning disabilities is the human brain itself. And we all have the same brain whether we use it in English or Chinese — the slight differences in personal conditioning between you and me, or cultural or religious or gender differences, are superficial. The biological brains of our species are as alike as the brains of two hummingbirds, give or take a couple of points of I.Q., give or take a couple of neurological impairments. So, generally speaking, the whole human species has some learning problems. Among them:

We seem only to use a small percent (10%-15%) of our brain capacity.

Of the brain's two capacities, insight (unlimited) and thought (limited), we overuse thought, which is limited to technology and cannot extend to a total understanding of ourselves and our relationship to the universe. Essentially, this means we all have a form of learning disability.

The biggest problem is that we see and hear only what our receptors are conditioned to see and hear, all physics to the contrary. For instance, we see form instead of energy and light (you and I and the table under my computer are just atoms in space, not you and I and a table), and we are preoccupied with things that don't exist; for example, self and psychological time (both invented by thought). Most of us have no notion that we see not what is there, but what our brains have been taught to see. And we suffer from shadows — try to hold your past or your future in the palm of your hand. Surely, these limitations are a learning disability common to us all.

Specific learning disabilities are real, and in our success-through-education-oriented society, they can be frightening and isolating. But before you develop prejudices about someone who can't spell, or focus for long on a book or conversation or career, someone for whom a cocktail party is a nightmare of social confusion, try to remember *all* human brains are still blundering about after millions of years of so-called evolution.

APPENDIX
SOURCES FOR HELP

AbleData, National Rehabilitation Information Center, The Catholic University of America, 4407 Eighth Street NE, Washington, DC 20017. (202) 635-5822

A.D.D.A. (Attention Deficit Disorder Association is a national alliance of support groups that provides referrals and information), 8091 South Ireland Way, Aurora, CO 80016. (800) 487-2282

Association on Handicapped Student Service Programs in Postsecondary Education (AHSSPPEE), Box 21192, Columbus, OH 43221. (614) 488-4972

C.H.A.D. Children with Attention Deficit Disorder, 499 70th Avenue N.W. #19, Plantation, FL 33317. (305) 587-3700

ERIC Clearinghouse on Disabilities and Gifted Education Council for Exceptional Children, 1920 Association Drive, Reston, VA 22091. (703) 620-3660

Learning Disabilities Association of America, Inc., 4156 Library Road, Pittsburgh, PA 15234. (412) 341-1515

National Center for Learning Disabilities, 381 Park Avenue S., New York, NY 10016. (212) 687-7211

National Information Center for Children and Youths with LD Academy for Educational Development, Box 1492, Washington, DC 20013. (202) 884-8200, (800) 695-0285

National Network of Learning Disabled Adults, 808 North 82nd Street, #F2, Scottsdale, AZ 85257. (602) 941-5112

Office of Vocational Rehabilitation Services, 330 C Street S.W., Switzer Bldg., Washington, DC 20202. (202) 205-9404

Orton Dyslexia Society, Chester Bldg, #382, 8600 La Salle Road, Towson, MD 21204. (410) 296-0232, (800) 222-3123

YOUNG ADULT AND ADULT EDUCATIONAL GUIDES

You can call your nearest college or university and ask for the Department of Special Education in the Graduate School of Education. Also, you can go to your library and look at:

Peterson's Colleges with Programs for Learning Disabled Students

Schoolsearch Guide to Colleges with Programs or Services for Students with Learning Disabilities

Also write to or call:

The Lab School of Washington, 4759 Reservoir Road NW, Washington, DC 20016. (202) 965-6600

Local School Systems

State Departments of Education

You can find further lists of organizations, information centers, research centers, resources for legal aid, funding, testing and diagnosis tools in the books recommended under selected reference bibliography.

SELECTED REFERENCE BIBLIOGRAPHY

Hallowell, Edward M., M.D. and Ratey, John J., M.D., *Driven to Distraction: Recognizing and Coping with Attention Deficit Disorder from Childhood through Adulthood*, New York, Pantheon Books, 1994.

Ingersoll, Barbara D., Ph.D. and Goldstein, Sam, Ph.D., *Attention Deficit Disorder and Learning Disabilities*, New York, Doubleday, 1993.

Knox, Jean McBee, *Learning Disabilities, The Encyclopedia of Health, Psychological Disorders and Their Treatment Series*, New York, Chelsea House Publishers, 1989.

Pueschel, Siegfried M., M.D., Scola, Patricia S., M.D., Weidenman, Leslie E., Ph.D., and Bernier, James C., A.C.S.W., *The Special Child: A Source Book for Parents of Children with Developmental Disabilities*, Paul H. Brookes Publishing Co., Baltimore, 1995.

Silver, Larry B., M.D., *The Misunderstood Child: A Guide for Parents of Children with Learning Disabilities — 2nd Edition*, New York, Tab Books, McGraw-Hill, Inc., 1992.

Smith, Sally L., *No Easy Answers: The Learning Disabled Child At Home and At School*, New York, Bantam Books, 1995.

Williams, Donna, *Somebody, Somewhere: Breaking Free from the World of Autism*, New York, Times Books, Random House, 1994.

There are children's books available on learning disabilities and ADHD.

There are also tapes and videos available as well as teaching films. Contact The Lab School of Washington, Products and Services Division, 4759 Reservoir Road N.W., Washington, DC 20007, (202) 965-6600.

Sally Smith's book *No Easy Answers* contains valuable appendices, with excellent lists of materials available, as well as organizations and advocacy groups, recommended professional journals, diagnostic tests, and much more that is useful and helpful to parents, families, friends, teachers of those with learning disabilities.